God,

Where Are You?

KIRKIE MORRISSEY

God, Where Are You?

Finding Your Faith

in Dark Times

NAVPRESS

Bringing Truth to Life
P.O. Box 35001, Colorado Springs, Colorado 80935

The Navigators is an international Christian organization. Our mission is to reach, disciple, and equip people to know Christ and to make Him known through successive generations. We envision multitudes of diverse people in the United States and every other nation who have a passionate love for Christ, live a lifestyle of sharing Christ's love, and multiply spiritual laborers among those without Christ.

NavPress is the publishing ministry of The Navigators. NavPress publications help believers learn biblical truth and apply what they learn to their lives and ministries. Our mission is to stimulate spiritual formation among our readers.

ISBN 1-57683-331-3

Cover Design: Kirk DouPonce, UDG|DesignWorks, www.udgdesignworks.com
Cover Photo: Clarissa Leahy, Stone
Creative Team: Brad Lewis, Amy Spencer, Glynese Northam

Some of the anecdotal illustrations in this book are true to life and are included with the permission of the persons involved. All other illustrations are composites of real situations, and any resemblance to people living or dead is coincidental.

All Scripture quotations in this publication are taken from the HOLY BIBLE: NEW INTERNATIONAL VERSION® (NIV®). Copyright © 1973, 1978, 1984 by International Bible Society. Used by permission of Zondervan Publishing House. All rights reserved.

Printed in the United States of America
1 2 3 4 5 6 7 8 9 10 / 06 05 04 03 02

Contents

Acknowledgments

Y EDITOR, BRAD LEWIS, DESERVES MANY THANKS FOR HIS HARD WORK EDITING
this manuscript. I greatly appreciate his expertise and kindness in
working with me, paring down and at times reformatting this material.
Coming alongside me in this project he expressed his support as he cri-
tiqued and edited the study: "My goal with directions for revisions is for
this simply to be a better study. I really like where you take readers on
this ride! I couldn't have even started them down the road. But I think I
can help you help them enjoy the ride a little more if you follow my sug-
gestions." I believe you're right, Brad. You've been a great "partner." Thank
you, too, to Amy Spencer, project coordinator. Good job!

Nanci McAlister, Author Relations Coordinator and Acquisitions
Editor at NavPress, has also been a great support and encourager from
the time she first reviewed this manuscript. In addition, as we've worked
together over the past few years on Bible studies, she has become a dear
friend. Her delightful sense of humor, honesty, and prayer support have
meant a lot to me as she's walked alongside me on some of the rough
roads of my journey from which this study came. As she's glimpsed my
pain, her compassion has ministered to me. Thank you, Nanci!

My precious daughter-in-law, Patti Morrissey, also deserves heartfelt
thanks. In addition to her love, her administrative support has helped me
tremendously. Patti lifted a tedious burden as she carried the load of
tracking down publishers and authors to obtain permissions for the many
quotes included in this study. As other administrative needs arose, she
willingly responded with skill, time, and energy. Patti is a great help, a very
special friend, and a dear daughter-in-law. She is a blessing and a gift from
the Lord — not just to me but to our family and many others as well.
Thank you, Patti. I love you and thank the Lord for you.

And as always, Ann, thank you for reviewing the first rough drafts of
my studies. Your willingness to drop what you're doing when a deadline
is pressing is gratefully acknowledged and appreciated. In addition, in light
of this study in particular, I thank you for your faithfulness to me as a
friend. Many times when I felt like I was "lying by the side of the road,"

emotionally stripped and beaten, you were "the good Samaritan" who picked me up and cared for me. Your prayers, love, and friendship have been a Godsend. You've been His gift and provision through the hardest journey of my life. Thank you, dear friend.

My Personal Journey

"WEEPING MAY REMAIN FOR A NIGHT," WROTE DAVID (PSALM 30:5). FOR ME, it was a long, dark night—an agonizing night that seemed to last forever. As I wept in the darkness, I wrestled with everything I believed in my faith.

Have you been there? Are you there now? If so, I'm sorry. Pain that brings such intense struggle is severe. I feel for you and pray that somehow what I learned in my journey helps you in yours. This study was born out of my own intense struggles.

The specific circumstances of my journey aren't important. What is important are the truths I discovered and the deep work the Lord did in me. Because this journey involves others I care about very much, I prefer not to share intimate details out of consideration for them. What God did through this journey is what matters. That I will share!

On the surface, my life looked fine—and much of it was. I had many things to smile about and to be thankful for. Of the things I was most thankful were my three precious sons. Also, I had a handsome husband who owned a successful construction business. He provided well for us— we were very comfortable. We had an abundance of friends, and our church was dynamic. But not everything was as rosy as it appeared. In my heart, I carried a lot of pain.

One aspect of my journey was that some hopes and dreams of a lifetime had died. I was confused because I had sought the Lord's leading in a major decision of my life and trusted Him, but later I discovered that all was not as I had thought. Had God betrayed me? This question haunted me.

As circumstances intensified through the years, what I thought couldn't get any worse, did! One day in the middle of a grocery store parking lot, I screamed piercingly at the top of my lungs, then cried out: "God!"

But the response was silence. Why wasn't God helping me? Didn't He love me? Didn't He care about my pain? If God is good, how could He simply look on and let me suffer? I'd always felt I could handle anything as long as Jesus was near. But now, *where was* He?

My journal entries went from "Lord, You are my Beloved! You are my life and my joy!" to "Where are You, Lord?" "How long before You speak to me, Lord, how long?" "Where is Your mercy?" "Where is Your love?" Tears stained the pages. The pain of His "absence" was almost more than I could bear.

Finally, after intense wrestling, I cried, "Uncle!" I decided that I would stop fighting God. Instead I begrudgingly yielded to Him. He had won. He needed to work in me—and deep down I knew it was necessary. Rather than continuing to resist, my heart changed and I began to pray for the Lord to use my pain for His good purposes. Suddenly I discovered that the pain was no longer destructive—it had become productive!

Every once in awhile, God would give me a glimpse of what He was quietly accomplishing in me, and I'd see it was good. My inner peace increased as a result. Slowly, some of the things I didn't like in myself and that were not pleasing to Him (like insidious pride, caring too much what people thought of me, and wanting my own will in many circumstances) were disappearing. In addition, I was discovering deeper truths of who God is and all He desires for me that far surpassed my previous understanding of Him. Somehow, too, my faith—which had been based more on feelings and sight—became firmly established on truth. I was amazed at what God was doing in the midst of my pain.

One day, a friend asked me, "If you had it to do over again, would you still make the same decision you made years ago?" That was major. Once again I had to wrestle with the same issue: "Had God betrayed me?" As I pondered my response to her question, it dawned on me: "Yes, I would!" Yes, because of all the Lord was doing in me, because of the deeper closeness I had with Jesus, because of the greater fullness of His Spirit I was beginning to experience, I exclaimed, "Yes!" Then I realized that God *knew* all along how I'd answer this question. He hadn't betrayed me. What joy!

Though the night continued longer (God had more work to do in me), I had a new assurance that any struggles I went through wouldn't last longer than necessary. God knew what He was doing—and it was good! Of course, it was still terribly painful. Yet I hung on to the hope expressed by David in Psalm 30:5: "Weeping may remain for a night, but rejoicing comes in the morning." Morning would come—someday. I would make it, by His grace and through His faithfulness. And it would be worth it all.

CHAPTER ONE

What Do I Do with My Questions?

H AVE CIRCUMSTANCES IN YOUR OWN LIFE OR SOMEONE ELSE'S EVER CAUSED you to question God's character? For example, has the pain of the death of someone you love cast doubts about God's goodness?

Or maybe you've suffered abuse and struggled with the question, "Why didn't God help me?"

In addition to personal difficulties, terrible events in the world might also challenge your faith. When the United States suffered the terrorist attacks on September 11, 2001, many people struggled, wondering, "Where was God?" In such times when circumstances and feelings seemingly contradict what we believe about God, what we do with our questions is critical.

We might feel guilty when we entertain questions concerning the character of God. Perhaps we fleetingly muse, "God, are You really good?" Then suddenly *guilt* surges through us and we think, "How terrible to consider such a thing!" Or perhaps we *fear* we'll discover that God isn't who we think He is. How threatening! So we quickly deny, ignore, or bury our doubts deep within.

Yet is it wrong to doubt? If we succumb to such doubts, do we need to feel guilty? More important, is there any reason to fear asking these hard questions? How would God have us handle the tough questions that plague us? Let's take an honest look at these issues.*

---

* Whether you do these Bible studies alone or with a group, the chapter divisions exist only to divide the topics. You might go faster than one chapter per week/session. More likely, you'll proceed more slowly. That's fine. In fact, rather than try to make each chapter exactly the same length or completely parallel, I've tried to cover each topic thoroughly, yet somewhat concisely. Take as much time as you need to completely and deeply explore each chapter's overall topic as well as the study questions contained in each chapter.

1. How do you typically respond to your own doubts about God? What about when others express their doubts? Can you give any examples?

2. As you consider the issue of doubts, it's important to examine various attitudes you might have about *asking questions.*

   A. What do you discover from each of the following passages? Record *who* was asking, what that person's *attitude* was, and what *resulted.*

      Matthew 22:15-22

      John 3:1-5

      John 18:37-38

      Acts 24:24-26

   B. Do you think people today have these same attitudes? Do you recognize any patterns in yourself? If so, what?

3. In Mark 9:30-32, the disciples didn't understand Jesus. Yet they were afraid to find out what He meant, so they didn't ask questions.

   A. What fears keep you from bringing your questions to the Lord? Be honest in identifying these.

   B. As you seek answers from God, you don't need to fear what you'll discover. Down through the ages, people who have truly sought God have found that *He is who He says He is*. (For example, consider Job's experience in Job 42:1-6, and Jeremiah's discoveries in Jeremiah 20:7-8 with 32:17-24.) Because you don't need to fear what you'll learn about God, what hope do you have?

4. Don't be afraid to honestly ask God your most challenging questions. Consider these examples of people who were courageous enough to ask.

   A. John the Baptist was a "miracle" baby. Fulfilling the promise of God, his parents conceived him way past their childbearing years. John's purpose was to go before Jesus, preparing "the way of the Lord." John identified Jesus as the Messiah, loudly proclaiming, "Look, the Lamb of God, who takes away the sin of the world!" (John 1:29). Read John 1:32-34 and Matthew 3:16-17. What proof did John have that Jesus truly was the Son of God?

      i. Despite all his assurances, when John the Baptist was imprisoned—facing death—he apparently doubted. Maybe he wondered, "If Jesus is the Christ, why isn't He rescuing me?" Read Luke 7:18-23. What did John do regarding his faith struggles? What was Jesus' response?

    ii. Does it help you to know that even John the Baptist wrestled with doubts in a difficult time? How does it help? How does Jesus' response to John's doubts encourage you?

B. Read John 20:24-29. In these verses you'll find the story of Thomas, one of Jesus' disciples. His struggle with doubt was so significant that a person today who doubts might still be called a "Doubting Thomas."

    i. As one of Jesus' twelve disciples, Thomas witnessed many miracles and heard Christ's teachings. But Thomas also witnessed Jesus' crucifixion. Even though the other disciples exclaimed they had seen Jesus, he didn't believe them. What condition did he put on his belief?

    ii. What did Jesus say when He appeared to Thomas? What was Thomas's response?

    iii. Does Thomas's experience encourage you? How? Be specific.

5. Perhaps you have some uncertainty about who God is, but you don't know specifically what your questions are. What do you learn from Jeremiah 17:10 and Luke 5:21-22?

A. How can the Lord help you with your questions? Consider Ephesians 5:13-14.

B. What are your responsibilities?

6. What questions do you have about the Lord or your faith? Record each here (or in a journal). Ask the Lord to lead you into truth regarding each question.

7. What does God *promise* in Isaiah 45:19 and Matthew 7:7-8?

A. Do you think you can count on these promises to be true for *you*? Why or why not?

B. As you continue to seek answers about your doubts, take time to thank God that He promises to meet you and lead you into truth.

REFLECTION/DISCUSSION QUESTIONS

1. What, if anything, has triggered doubts in you? What have you done with your doubts and questions?

2. What are some reasons people hold on to their doubts? What do you think the consequences are of not facing our doubts or of not seeking the truth about them?

3. Why is honesty an essential attribute as we seek God's truth? What do you think occurs when we're not honest with God?

4. Does anything from this lesson encourage you to ask your toughest questions? Below, or in a journal, list the one thought or Scripture passage from this lesson that helped you the most.

CHAPTER TWO

Whom Can I Go to for Truth?

"**G**O TO THE SOURCE!" HAVE YOU EVER HEARD THAT ADVICE? IF YOU WANT TO gather information or gain understanding, finding the original source is the best way to make sure you're getting things right.

For example, if I got to choose whom to ask about a problem with a Microsoft program on my computer, I'd prefer the input of the author and designer of the software over the advice of a friend.

Do we have that option regarding life itself? Can we go to the Source? As we pursue answers to our questions, is it possible to really know truth? We may even wonder, "Is truth relative, or do some absolutes exist? Is there a final authority for questions pertaining to God and the issues of life? Is there a Creator who communicates the knowledge we desire?"

These are critical issues to consider. If we can't trust in an absolute authority, we'll never be sure that we're basing our life on absolute truth. So, let's pursue whether or not there is Someone we can go to who will lead us into what is absolutely true.

1. As you think about our culture, the media, and even people around you, what attitudes do you see regarding the existence of an absolute authority about the truth?

2. If there is a living God, do you think He is the true authority? Why or why not?

   A. Read Romans 14:11 and Revelation 1:8,17-18. What does the Lord reveal about His existence?

   B. What evidence do the following verses provide about the reality of a living God?

   Jeremiah 10:10

   Daniel 6:25-27

   1 Timothy 3:15

   C. Are you aware of any other evidence that supports the existence of a living God?

3. Christians believe that Jesus Christ is God, and therefore He's the authority on life and spiritual issues. What's the foundation for such a belief and how strong is it? Consider the following.

A. What testimony is given about Jesus Christ in each of the following verses? Record your discoveries and meditate on each.

Matthew 3:16-17

John 1:1-4,14-18

Colossians 1:15-20

B. What does Jesus claim about His deity in Luke 22:70 and John 8:54-58, 10:30, and 16:28-30?

C. Jesus gave evidence of His deity and authority as He walked on earth. In what areas does He exhibit His authority in each of the following verses? What does each Scripture passage communicate about His deity?

Luke 4:33-36 (also 4:40-41)

Luke 5:22–26

Luke 8:22–25

D. In John 14:6 and 18:37, what does Jesus claim regarding truth?

    i. Read John 3:3, 5:19, and 10:7–10. What phrase does Jesus often use in His teaching?

    ii. In John 12:49–50, where does He say His teaching comes from?

    iii. What claim does He make about His words in Matthew 24:35?

    iv. What do His claims communicate to you?

4. Some people believe that Jesus was just a good man or a great teacher. Author Josh McDowell provides some thoughts about this in *More Than a Carpenter*:

> C. S. Lewis, who was a professor at Cambridge University and once an agnostic, understood this issue clearly. He writes: "I am trying here to prevent anyone from saying the really foolish thing that people often say about Him: 'I'm ready to accept Jesus as a great moral teacher, but I don't accept His claim to be God.' That is the one thing we must not say. A man who was merely a man and said the sort of things Jesus said would not be a great moral teacher. He would either be a lunatic ...or else he would be the Devil of Hell. You must make your choice. Either this man was, and is, the Son of God: or else a madman or something worse."

McDowell then adds, "Jesus claimed to be God. He didn't leave any other option open. His claim must be either true or false."[1]

What are your thoughts about who Jesus was (and is)? What do you base these on?

5. As you continue to explore the issue that Jesus is God and that He always spoke the truth, consider that He came as the sinless Lamb of God to be the sacrifice for all sin. See John 1:29 and 1 Peter 1:18-21.

   A. Do you think Jesus would have been qualified to be God's sacrificial Lamb if He had said even one thing that wasn't absolutely true? Explain.

B. Consider Revelation 5:6-12. Did He fulfill His purpose as the Lamb of God?

C. What does this say to you about whether Jesus' statements are accurate and trustworthy?

6. Jesus' predictions about His future provide further proof of His deity and His embodiment of truth. Prior to His death, Jesus told His disciples that He would be crucified, and on the third day be raised back to life. It happened, just as He said. (See Luke 24:1-8,25-27,36-49.) What does this mean to you?

7. Jesus promised that He would send the Holy Spirit when He was seated once again at the right hand of His Father (see John 16:5-7). Did this occur? How does this demonstrate that Jesus is God and that He does speak truth? See Luke 24:49-53 and Acts 2:1-4,32-33. Consider this thoughtfully.

8. After Jesus' resurrection and ascension into heaven, Stephen's experience gives added support to the truth that Jesus is alive. Stephen, active in the early church, was "a man full of God's grace and power [who] did great wonders and miraculous signs among the people"

(Acts 6:8). Read Acts 7:54-56. The leaders of the Sanhedrin unleashed their anger on Stephen after he spoke strongly against them. At that moment, what did Stephen experience that verifies the truths you're exploring here?

9. Like Stephen and Thomas, some people have dramatic encounters with Christ in their journeys. Others have more quiet discoveries of truth. What observations or experiences from your life communicate to *you* that Jesus is God and that He's the authority for life? Do any other thoughts cause you to question this? Explain.

10. Look at Matthew 17:1-5. What does God exhort us to do when He proclaims that Jesus is His Son? What does this mean to you?

> Dr. Martyn Lloyd-Jones says, "The whole of the New Testament is clearly designed to convince us of the authority of Jesus Christ. It is clear that if He is not who He claims to be, there is no need to listen to Him. If He is, then we are bound to listen to Him." [2]

What is your response to this thought?

ℛEFLECTION/𝒟ISCUSSION 𝒬UESTIONS

1. What struggles or resistance do you think people have for believing that a true authority for life exists? If such an authority truly exists, what would it mean? As you reflect on the evidence explored in this chapter, what are your thoughts? What's your response to the reality of a living God as the true authority?

2. What questions do you guess some people have about Jesus being God and that He's this authority? Who do you think Jesus is? Why? What evidence considered in this chapter meant the most to you?

3. As you ask difficult questions about life, what do you find in this study that encourages you to look for truth?

4. What hope do these discoveries give you for your life? Explain.

CHAPTER THREE

Can I Trust God's Word?

IS THE BIBLE SIMPLY A BOOK OF GOOD TEACHINGS OR A COMPILATION OF LITERATURE? Or is it the Word of God?

Does it simply offer "good advice"? Or is it our resource for absolute truth?

If God Himself is Truth and our authority, as explored in the previous chapter, does the Bible contain God's words of truth?

This is a critical issue to explore. It's essential because the Bible not only states who God is, but it also assures us that His promises are true. Can God's words in the Bible be trusted? Let's consider this matter carefully.

1. What views do you think others hold regarding the Bible?

    A. What's your own opinion of the Bible? Why?

    B. Do you have questions regarding the Bible's authority and trust-
       worthiness?

2. As you explore whether or not the Bible as the Word of God is truth, a foundational issue to consider is the character of God.

A. What truth is stated in Isaiah 45:19 and Titus 1:2?

B. Reflect on this attribute of God. What does this mean to you?

3. The Bible makes specific claims regarding its truth. Consider the following.

A. In Psalms 12:6, 33:4, and 119:160, what is stated about the words of God?

B. What does Jesus state in John 17:17 regarding the truth of the Bible?

> Dr. John R. W. Stott writes, "The central issue relates, therefore, not to the authority of the Bible, but to the authority of Christ. If *he* accepted the Old Testament as God's Word, are we going to reject it? . . . To reject the authority of either the Old Testament or the New Testament is to reject the authority of Christ." [1]

What do you think about this statement?

C. What quality of God's Word is mentioned in Isaiah 40:8? What does Jesus say about this in Matthew 24:35? What does this say to you about trusting God's Word?

D. Read 2 Timothy 3:14-16. What specific claim is made in verse 16 regarding the value of "all Scripture"?

4. Other evidence proving that Scripture is the Word of God is seen in the following:

A. What claim do the prophets make regarding the words they spoke? See Isaiah 45:18-19 and Jeremiah 29:10-11, 30:1-3.

B. Jesus clearly stated that the Scriptures are truth (John 17:17). What profound revelation does He make concerning the Word of God in the section of dialogue recorded in John 10:35?

C. Read John 14:26. What promise did Jesus give His disciples in this verse? How is the truth of this confirmed in 1 Corinthians 2:6-13? What does this tell you about the books of the New Testament?

D. What conviction does the apostle Paul express in 1 Thessalonians 2:13? What endorsement does the apostle Peter give in 2 Peter 1:20-21?

Lloyd-Jones further substantiates the fact that the whole Bible came from God in "the remarkable harmony between the Old and New Testaments, and the perfect and final agreement between all its books. In the Bible there are sixty-six books written over one thousand six hundred years by more than forty writers, and yet, virtually, they are all saying the same thing." In addition, he states, "There are scientific arguments, historical arguments, archaeological arguments and rational arguments, which have been adduced in support of the authority of the Scriptures."[2]

Josh McDowell in *The New Evidence That Demands a Verdict* adds further support of the truth and authority of the Scriptures through the documentation of fulfilled prophecy. McDowell quotes two authorities, Geisler and Nix, stating: "Other books claim divine inspiration . . . but none of those books contain predictive prophecy." They continue: "No unconditional prophecy of the Bible about events to the present day has gone unfilled. Hundreds of predictions, some of them given hundreds of years in advance, have been literally fulfilled." After citing example after example, they conclude: "As a result, fulfilled prophecy is a strong indication of the unique, divine authority of the Bible."[3]

What effect do these statements have on your thinking?

5. Read the verses below. How are the words of God proven to be true in these incidents?

Exodus 6:2-8 with Joshua 21:43-45

Nehemiah 9:8

Matthew 1:20-23 and 2:13-15,21-23

6. Consider the following explanations regarding how the truth of Jesus being *the incarnate Word of God* relates to the Bible:

Oswald Chambers wrote,

Our Lord Jesus Christ (the Word of God) and the Bible (the accompanying revelation) stand or fall together; they can never be separated without fatal results . . . It is not a question of the infallibility of the Bible — that is a side issue — but of the finality of the Bible. The Bible is a whole library of literature giving us the final interpretation of the truth, and to take the Bible apart from that one supreme purpose is to have a book and nothing more . . . "The Truth" is our Lord Himself, "the whole truth" is the inspired Scripture interpreting the Truth to us, and "nothing but the truth" is the Holy Spirit, "the Spirit of truth," efficaciously regenerating and sanctifying us and guiding us into all truth (John 16:13).[4]

A. W. Tozer expounded on Jesus as the Word of God and how this relates to the written Scriptures:

*A word is a medium by which thoughts are expressed, and the appli-
cation of the term to the Eternal Son leads us to believe that self-
expression is inherent in the Godhead . . . The whole Bible supports
the idea. God is speaking. Not God spoke, but God is speaking . . . It
is the present Voice which makes the written Word all-powerful . . . The
Bible is the inevitable outcome of God's continuous speech.*

Tozer then exhorts us: "If you would follow on to know
the Lord, come at once to the open Bible expecting it to
speak to you. Do not come with the notion that it is a *thing*
which you may push around at your convenience. It is more
than a thing, it is a voice, a word, the very Word of the living God." [5]

Are any of the promises in the above statements particularly meaningful to you?

7. Applying God's truth to our lives involves *two aspects.*

A. We can *always* apply the truths of *who He is.*

i. What qualities of God do you find in the following passages?

Deuteronomy 32:4

Psalm 145:8-9,17-18

Jeremiah 31:3

Romans 8:38-39

Hebrews 13:5

ii. Are there qualities of His that you have doubted, or that you currently question? How do your discoveries from this chapter encourage you?

iii. Because of His character, what are we exhorted to do in Psalm 62:8?

B. We can also apply the truths of *what God will do*. This is where many people get confused regarding the character of God. Sometimes people will take a Scripture passage indicating what God *can* do, or *did* do, and claim that is what He *will* do in a specific instance in their life. But then if He doesn't do what they thought He would do in that specific circumstance, they conclude that His Word isn't true. For example, in Luke 8:50, Jesus told a father that if he believed, his daughter would be healed. This was Jesus' promise to this one man. However, believing that Jesus can still do this today, people may take this passage and claim it for their own loved one. And of course, while the Lord does choose to heal people today, there are other times when, for reasons unknown to us, He doesn't do so. In such times, people can become disillusioned in their faith and conclude that God is not true or faithful to His Word.

    i. Have you ever had an experience like the one above that caused you to question the truth of God's Word? Does the principle of depending on who He *is* rather than what He will *do* help you? How?

    ii. Reflect on Jeremiah 23:16-18. What do we need to do to discern what God's promise is in a specific circumstance?

    iii. When God does give a specific promise, what can we count on? In addition to what you've studied in this lesson, consider Abraham's conviction recorded in Romans 4:18-21.

8. Finally, what does the psalmist state about God's Word in Psalm 119:105? Does this mean anything for your life?

Thank God for providing His Word for you.

REFLECTION/DISCUSSION QUESTIONS

1. As we seek the truth, what do you think carries the greatest weight: Man's reason or God's Word? Lloyd-Jones states, "The modern position amounts to this, that it is man's reason that decides . . . Man's knowledge and man's understanding are the final arbiters and the final court of appeal." [6] Why do people seem to put more confidence in themselves or others than in God? What do you tend to base your beliefs on? Why?

2. If God is the living God (as explored in the previous chapter), wouldn't He want to communicate His truth regarding life to the people He created? What would God be like if He did *not* want to communicate with His creation? What does this say to you?

3. What discoveries from this chapter influenced your thinking the most about whether or not God's Word is truth? Explain.

   A. Is anything keeping you from accepting that the entire Bible is truth—that it is the authoritative Word of God? If so, explain. How will you pursue finding the answers to your questions?

   B. If the Bible truly is the inspired Word of God, what does this mean to you? How does this help you as you continue your journey of seeking truth?

4. When taking a road trip to a new place, people follow a map. If you purchase a new piece of equipment, such as a VCR, you can learn to use it correctly by reading the instruction manual. Why do you think, for something as important as life itself, people often prefer to find their own way rather than going to the Bible, or to the Author of Life, for directions?

5. As you reflect on your discoveries in this lesson, what difference will it make in how you approach God's Word and in the authority you allow it to have in your life regarding who God is, insights into your questions, and what life is about? Be specific.

CHAPTER FOUR

"Lord, Do You Love Me?"

WHEN PRAYERS SEEM TO GO UNANSWERED, WHEN DIFFICULTIES SEEM UNEND-ing, do you wonder, "Does God love me?" If you're a parent, when your child cries to you for help, you immediately respond out of your love for him. So, when your cries to the Lord seemingly go unheeded, you might question God's love. Or perhaps you weren't loved by your parents, so you wonder, "How could God possibly love me?"

Circumstances can cause us to question God's love for us, and com-paring ourselves with others can also stir up feelings of inadequacy. We may wonder if the Lord loves us as much as He does someone who seems to be more talented, more attractive, or more intelligent. Deep within, we may be thinking, "I can see why You would love *her*! But do you love *me*?" In addition, guilt over things we have done may make it difficult to believe that the Lord could love us or desire a close relationship with us.

These are important feelings to explore. If we don't look for answers to the questions we have about God's love for us, this will not only cre-ate barriers to growing in our relationship with God, but will also create obstacles to knowing who we are. Resolving these issues is important personally and spiritually.

1. Have you observed others who question whether or not the Lord loves them and desires a relationship with them? What causes these emotions? Is there anything that creates struggles for you in this area?

2. What are the *facts*? It's important for faith to be grounded on the truth of God's love and not be determined by our "feelings." What do the following Scriptures proclaim?

   A. What is God's heart for *you*, as expressed in John 17:22-23,26 and 1 John 3:1?

   B. Does God love *all* (therefore *you*)? See John 3:16-17.

   C. Read Ephesians 2:4-9 and 1 Timothy 1:12-17. Is God's love based on an assumption of merit? Is His love conditional? After reflecting on these truths, is there any basis for thinking God does not love you? Explain. Even if this is still difficult to accept, start by celebrating His declared love for you.

3. To further verify the truth of the Lord's love for you, consider what Christ did to prove His love.

   A. What do you discover in Romans 5:8 and 1 John 4:7-10? (Review John 3:16-17 also.) Each time you doubt God's love, look at the cross. When Jesus gave His life for you, He proved His love. Take time now to meditate on His incredible gift of love.

   B. How does it affect you to see the extent that God went to in order to prove His love and provide a way for you to have a relationship with Him? Express your heart to Him in this.

   C. If, after exploring these evidences of God's love, you still have difficulty believing that He loves you, write down some reasons why you have a hard time accepting this fact. Express your heart to God. Tell Him of your doubts and concerns. Ask Him for insight, as He knows you completely. Ask Him to remove any barriers that are keeping you from receiving or responding to His love. Then review the facts of His love explored in this study so far.

4. In addition to the above evidences of His love, consider also God's role in your very existence.

   A. What do you discover in the following verses?

      Psalms 100:3

      Psalm 119:73

      Psalm 139:13-16

      Isaiah 44:24

      Isaiah 64:8

B. How does Revelation 4:11 confirm this?

C. Is this a new discovery to you? Reflect on this truth. What does it mean to realize how special you are to God?

D. If the essence of God's nature is love, what would be the attitude of His heart toward someone He created? For insight, think of how you feel toward something you have a vested, personal interest in.

E. Reflect also on Isaiah 49:15-16. How does this expression of God's care make you feel?

F. In his book *Life of the Beloved*, Henri Nouwen expressed these truths from Scripture:

> From all eternity, long before you were born and became a part of history, you existed in God's heart . . . The eyes of love had seen you as precious, as of infinite beauty, as of eternal value . . . Long before

any person spoke to us in this world, we are spoken to by the voice of eternal love. Our preciousness, uniqueness and individuality are not given to us by those who meet us in clock-time — our brief chronological existence — but by the One who has chosen us with an everlasting love, a love that existed from all eternity and will last through all eternity.[1]

Reflect on these realities. Ponder how special you are to Him.

5. However, if Jesus died for all, does that mean every person automatically has a relationship with God? Consider John 3:3-7, Romans 10:8-14, and Revelation 3:20.

   A. List reasons why you think it's essential that every person has a choice to follow Jesus.

   B. Nouwen portrayed God's desire for this relationship beautifully as he explained:

   The unfathomable mystery of God is that God is a Lover who wants to be loved. The one who created us is waiting for our response to the love that gave us our being. God not only says: "You are my Beloved," God also asks: "Do you love me?" . . . We are sent into this world for a short time to say . . . the great "Yes" to the love that has been given to us and in so doing return to the One who sent us with that "Yes" engraved on our hearts.[2]

   If you have not previously done so, why not say "Yes" to God's great love right now? If you desire this love relationship with your Creator and your Savior, express this to Him now. As you do so, what does He *promise* you, expressed in Revelation 3:20? Give Him thanks!

6. Our heavenly Father's unconditional love is beautifully portrayed in Jesus' parable of the prodigal son. Read Luke 15:11-24. Put yourself in the place of this prodigal, even if your actions have not been as overtly rebellious (and especially if they have!). Because our hearts are not pure and our actions are not perfect, we all in one way or another are like this prodigal. When you come to the Lord at any time, what can you count on based on Jesus' teaching here?

> Jerry Bridges writes in his book *Transforming Grace* (subtitled "Living Confidently in God's Unfailing Love"): "The realization that my daily relationship with God is based on the infinite merit of Christ instead of my own performance is a very freeing and joyous experience . . . Remember, that grace is either absolutely free, or it is not at all." Bridges then quotes Samuel Storms: "Grace is not grace if God is compelled to withdraw it in the presence of human demerit." Bridges continues, "Nothing you ever do or don't do will make God love you any more or any less"![3]

What is your response to the amazing grace (undeserved favor) of God?

7. In addition to simply acknowledging the facts of His love and grace, we need to take another essential step to allow them to root within and change our lives. We need to *accept* their truth and actively *receive* God's love and grace. In other words, these facts need to move from our heads down into our hearts. Take time now to appropriate His love and grace for yourself. Say (even out loud), "I *receive* Your love, Lord. Thank You!" Consciously accept it; then savor His love and grace. Most amazingly, you can live daily in these realities.

8. In closing, record here the truths you find in Romans 8:38-39. Personalize them. Rest in these truths and praise God for His promises.

$\mathscr{R}$EFLECTION/$\mathscr{D}$ISCUSSION $\mathscr{Q}$UESTIONS

1. Instead of believing that God is a God of love, what other concepts do people sometimes hold about God? What do you think these perceptions are based on? What images or perceptions of God have you held in the past? What did you base your thoughts on?

2. Even as you recognize God's incredible love, do you sometimes find it hard to accept His love? Why do people struggle in accepting God's love? Do you have difficulty receiving Jesus' love? Why? Did any truths from this chapter help you in this? Be specific.

3. Are the difficulties you might have receiving His love also true for receiving His grace—His unmerited forgiveness? Explain. What occurs when we allow our guilt to keep us from coming to the Lord? What truths will help you come to Him, confident of His unconditional love and grace?

4. What are some steps you can take to help root these wonderful, freeing truths of God's love and grace in your heart, so that you can live in their realities each day? Be specific and practical. What have you personally found helpful?

CHAPTER FIVE

"Lord, Do You Know Every Detail of My Life— and Do You Care?"

L IFE CAN BE CHALLENGING! THE DEMANDS WE FACE ARE NUMEROUS AND THE CIR-cumstances we go through are almost never simple. When difficulties occur, it seems impossible to tell our friends exactly what we're feeling or what's going on. While they might sympathize, they can't fully comprehend what we're experiencing.

It's easy to feel alone with our problems. Perhaps we pray and pray about each circumstance. But if very little changes, we might even wonder if God is aware of what we're going through. Can anything be hidden from God? Do things happen without His awareness? "Does He know everything, not only in my life but also in my heart?" we ask longingly.

In addition, if we desire God's wisdom in situations or want to trust Him with our lives, we need assurance that He's totally knowledgeable regarding every aspect. To trust Him, to accept His counsel, to rest in His care, we need to be confident that "God knows."

And we also want to know that He cares. In times when things seem to go from bad to worse, these heart issues become very significant. How often we may cry, "Lord, do You *know*? Lord, do you *care*?" Let's look for the truth about God's love and care for us.

1. What fears can people have if they don't believe that God knows their circumstances or deepest feelings? Do you personally struggle with any of these fears?

2. Look at the following Scriptures. What basic assurance of God's awareness do you find in these verses?

Job 34:21

Proverbs 5:21

Jeremiah 23:24

3. Read Hagar's experience in Genesis 16:1-14.

   A. Who was Hagar? What feelings existed between her and Sarai? What indicates that the Lord knew Hagar's circumstances?

   B. What name did Hagar give to the Lord?

C. Can you think of any ways that you're like Hagar? How do her experience and the name she gives God encourage you?

4. Does God know every detail concerning you? What does David proclaim in Psalm 139:1-6? Apply each verse specifically to yourself. How do you respond to these truths?

   A. Read on in Psalm 139:7-12. According to these verses, can you think of anywhere you can be that God isn't with you—or any circumstances so dark that He doesn't see what you're going through? Meditate on these truths, and take comfort in them.

   B. Have you ever been keenly aware of God's knowledge of you—your needs, your feelings, and/or your movements—on a certain day or in a particular circumstance? Give a specific example.

5. What do you discover in Psalm 38:9? Meditate on this truth. Come before Him now with your heart's sighs and spirit's deep longings. Allow Him to tenderly meet you.

6. Based on the evidence and testimony in this chapter so far, what are your thoughts about God's total awareness of you and your life?

    A. What does this specifically mean to you today?

    B. If you apply these truths about God's awareness to the people you love, how does it help you in your concerns for them?

7. Okay, so the Lord is aware of our problems and how we're hurting in our circumstances. But if we're not experiencing the help we'd like to have from Him, we might wonder, "Does He *care*?" Have you ever struggled with such feelings? If so, express your heart to Him honestly regarding these experiences.

    A. Read John 11:1-15. When Mary and Martha sent word to Jesus to help when their brother Lazarus was dying, He delayed leaving for two days. When Lazarus died, they may have questioned His knowledge of their situation and wondered about His love for them. After all, they had seen Jesus heal strangers, and they were such close friends of His. Why wouldn't He come immediately? What do you discover of Jesus' heart for them and His knowledge of their situation? What assurance does that give you if and when the Lord doesn't respond immediately to your cry for help?

B. What truths are revealed in Isaiah 40:25-31? How do these relate to your concerns about God's care for you?

C. Read Psalm 34:18. What further encouragement do you see here regarding God's care for you when you're hurting?

8. As we realize that God is who He proclaims Himself to be, we gain insight into the depth of His care for us. Read Isaiah 54:5 and 62:5. According to these verses, who is God to His people?

A. Who is Jesus? Consider John the Baptist's testimony regarding Christ in John 3:29 and Jesus' own testimony in Luke 5:34-35.

B. J. I. Packer stated,

> God's love to sinners involves His identifying Himself with their welfare. Such an identification is involved in all love: it is, indeed, the test of whether love is genuine or not . . . If a husband remains unmoved when his wife is in distress, we wonder at once how much love there can be in their relationship . . . So it is with God in His love for man . . . It is not for nothing that the Bible habitually speaks of God as the loving Father and Husband of His people.[1]

What's your response to the truth that God is a Husband to you with all of His qualities (for example, He is your loving, kind, faithful, good Husband)?

C. If you accept that God is the perfect Husband to you, what does it say about His care for you when you are hurting? What specific needs and longings does this help you deal with and surrender to His care?

Stop a moment and savor these truths of His love and care. In times when you question whether or not the Lord cares for you in your distress or cares about your pain, remember who God is to you.

9. In 1 Peter 5:7, what does Peter exhort you to do with your concerns and anxieties?

A. What does the word "cast," or "throw," convey to you?

B. Why does Peter say we can do this? Meditate on this awesome fact.

10. Read Philippians 4:4-7. What instruction does the apostle Paul give in these verses about your anxieties? What results as you do this?

    A. Below or in a journal, list each situation where you're hurting. Pray about each one of these circumstances. As you come to God, know that He is fully aware of every detail about your situation, He knows your feelings, and He cares for you.

    B. After praying about each hurt or anxiety, cast each concern upon the Lord. Repeat this every time you start to become anxious.

11. According to Matthew 6:6-8, when you take the steps above, what does Jesus assure you will happen ? Give God thanks.

REFLECTION/DISCUSSION QUESTIONS

1. What do you allow to influence your assurance of God's presence, knowledge, and love? For example, are you likely to let how a situation looks or how you feel in a crisis moment determine what you think is true? What steps can you take to overcome these tendencies, which undermine the reality of God's love and care for you? How can you better hold on to truth in the midst of challenging circumstances? Be specific.

2. How does it make you feel to know that God is aware of everything about you? In other words, does this encourage you, or make you uncomfortable, or both? How does it help to know that you don't need to explain to God all that's happening or what you're feeling? Compare this to having lunch with a friend and trying to explain the details of a troubling circumstance and your feelings about it.

3. Can you think of times when you were aware of God's complete knowledge of you? Think of ways that reviewing those times might help you in current or future circumstances.

4. What example or passage in Scripture from this lesson most encouraged you? What truths convinced you that the Lord not only knows what's going on in your life, but that He also cares?

5. Do you have any trouble grasping the truth that the Lord is Husband to you? Since He's not present in a physical sense, what do you think this concept means? How does this truth help you in troubled times? What are your responsibilities for allowing Him to demonstrate this quality in your life?

6. Do the truths of this lesson help you regarding your concerns for those you love? How? Be specific.

CHAPTER SIX

"Lord, Are You Really Good?"

"OF COURSE GOD IS GOOD," YOU MIGHT RESPOND. "IT'S A FACT."
You know in your head what the answer is "supposed" to be. But in your heart, do you sometimes wonder if it's true that God is good? Have things in your life caused you to question God's goodness?

Perhaps you've felt guilty admitting this doubt. Most of us feel we shouldn't question God's goodness. Yet, if we do not face our doubts, they can subtly erode the foundation of our faith. Besides, the Lord knows the questions that nag within us, and He desires for us to come to Him with them. God can stand the tough questions! Down through the ages, He's stood the test.

Because the Lord invites us to turn to Him, and because He longs for us to know who He truly is, let's bring Him our struggles and turn to His Word, seeking truth.

1. What types of events can cause people to question God's character and wonder if He is truly good? Have you personally struggled with this issue? If so, what has caused you to question God's goodness? Before you continue, express your feelings to God here, and ask Him to reveal truth to you.

2. What testimony regarding the character of God do you find in the passages below?

    A. Is God capable of evil or wrongdoing? Reflect on these passages:

    Deuteronomy 32:4

    Psalm 92:15

    1 John 1:5

    B. What's proclaimed about God's goodness in Psalm 100:4-5 and Jeremiah 33:11?

3. Moses walked closely with God. When he asked to see God's glory in Exodus 33:18-19,22, what word does God use interchangeably with His "glory"? What does it communicate to you that these words are used synonymously?

4. Jesus knows the Father completely. In fact, we have already discovered that Jesus, as the Lamb of God, could not have said anything that was not true. When you read Jesus' claim that only God is good in Matthew 19:17, how does it strengthen your faith that this statement *has* to be true?

  A. What does Jesus reveal about the Father in Matthew 7:7-11?

  B. Read Luke 23:44-46. What does it mean to you that even when Jesus was suffering on the cross, facing death, and experiencing separation from His Father, He still entrusted Himself to God the Father?

5. The book of Revelation provides a glimpse of what will occur at the end of time. Read Revelation 5:11-14.

  A. What testimony is given about Jesus Christ, the Lamb of God?

  B. What is the response to who He is?

C. Since this event occurs at the end of the world—after all has been done through all of time—what does it tell you regarding the constant goodness of God? Could Jesus be worshiped if He had ever done anything wrong? Explain. Recall this truth when you are struggling.

D. Corrie ten Boom absolutely believed in God's goodness at *all* times. After her release from Ravensbruk, the infamous women's concentration camp, the Lord granted her a powerful worldwide ministry. Many years later, when Corrie was eighty-five years old, she was given the gift of her first home. Billy Graham relates a story that one day "as her friend and movie director, the late Jimmy Collier, was leaving her home, he said, 'Corrie, hasn't God been good to give you this beautiful place?' She replied firmly, 'Jimmy, God was good when I was in Ravensbruk, too.'"[1]

Is this your view of God?

6. What's your initial response to the following question, and why: Do you think God is good to *everyone*?

A. What do you discern from Psalm 145:9,17 and Matthew 5:43-48?

B. What do you think keeps people from recognizing God's goodness to them? Is there anything that hinders you now or has hindered you in the past?

7. In light of God's goodness, do you think a Christian's life is always rosy? Consider the dimension of God's goodness revealed in Hebrews 12:5-11. As you reflect on the illustration of a good father with his son, what insight do you gain? Give an example from your own experience either as a child or as a parent.

A. Review Hebrews 12:10-11. What good results in our lives through God's wise and loving discipline?

B. How have you seen the goodness of God's discipline in your own life? How did you observe His goodness even if the discipline was painful at the time?

8. Read 2 Samuel 22:31-33 and Matthew 5:48. What word is used to sum up the essence of God's character in these verses? How does this encourage you?

9. When the Lord seems to allow people who are "not good" to continue in their waywardness, do you struggle with how God can be good? Read 2 Peter 3:9. Why does God exercise patience? What do you think this reveals about God's goodness?

10. How is God's wisdom described in James 3:17?

   A. How does God's wisdom seem to guide or direct His goodness? As you answer, think about the difference between God's "highest good" and the "immediate good."

   B. Can you think of a time when God's wisdom determined His actions as He gave you what was best—even if you didn't understand it at the time?

   C. How do these truths help you in anything you are currently experiencing? Apply them specifically.

11. How have your discoveries about God's qualities and character helped strengthen your confidence in His perfect goodness? How does knowing that He is good help you in your specific struggles?

12. In what areas do you desire to see and really know God's goodness? Express your heart to Him.

13. Read Isaiah 26:3. Because of who God is, what does this verse promise will occur as you trust Him? Give God thanks for who He is.

REFLECTION/DISCUSSION QUESTIONS

1. Do you think most people tend to think of God's goodness in terms of health, riches, and ease in living? Often people like to think of God as an indulgent grandfather who pats us on the head and doles out blessings. What insights into a truly good Father-God did you receive through this study?

2. What discoveries did you find particularly helpful about the character of God and your questions regarding His goodness? Be specific.

3. Does realizing that God's goodness is guided by His wisdom help you trust Him when you don't understand what He's doing? How? What circumstances does this realization help you deal with today?

4. What touches of God's goodness have you experienced in your life? Share the stories of His kindness, compassion, and goodness with someone else, remembering to give God the praise.

CHAPTER SEVEN

Why Do Bad Things Happen to Me?

GOD IS GOOD!

Of course, as soon as you make that statement, someone will ask, "Then why do terrible things occur, such as wars, abuse, accidents, disease, death?" In fact, you might even be asking, "I belong to God, so why do they happen to me?"

Is God responsible? Can He do evil? This chapter explores some of the *sources* of the pain we experience in life. If you're suffering, there aren't any easy answers; but there are helpful insights from Scripture that can provide some understanding—as well as real hope—in the midst of your pain or sorrow. To explore these issues, let's turn to God's Word.

1. First, it's important to see that our God does not callously observe from a distance the suffering and sorrow that occur on Earth.

   A. In each of the following passages, what do you discover that encourages you about God's involvement in your life?

   Psalm 56:8

   Isaiah 63:9

John 11:33-35

B. Read Paul's exhortation to Christians in Romans 12:15. What insight does this give you into God's heart?

C. Scripture reveals the incredible truth that God has *emotions*. For example, we've studied that He is loving. A further endorsement that He has emotions is that we are created in His image—and *we* have emotions. Read Jeremiah 48:31-32. What feelings does the Lord Himself express here? How does seeing God hurt affect you?

Joni Eareckson Tada has had many tears since the injury that left her confined to a wheelchair. As she has taken her questions and her sorrow to God, she's discovered that God truly cares. The title of one of her recent books reflects this: *When God Weeps*. She states:

When God Weeps is not so much about affliction as it is about the only One who can unlock sense out of suffering. It's not why our afflictions matter to us (although they do), but why they matter to the Almighty . . . "Weeping endures for a night, but joy comes in the morning": joy for those who suffer—but especially for God . . . My prayer [is] that through this book you will better understand why our weeping matters to a loving God. A God who, one day, will make clear the meaning behind every tear. Even his tears.[1]

How do Joni's thoughts encourage you?

2. As Jesus weeps with those who suffer, He is also *angered* by the evil in this world that hurts those He loves. Just as we feel angry at evil, so does our righteous God.

   A. Read the account of Jesus at Lazarus's tomb in John 11:33–39. Os Guinness discloses that the gospel writer, John, stated three times that Jesus was "furious." (Two different Greek words are used for Jesus being "deeply moved in spirit and troubled." See verses 33,38.) Guinness explains that these words reveal that Jesus was "indignant, livid, outraged, furious." The picture given by one word is that of a warhorse ready to charge into battle, rearing up on its hind legs and "snorting." Guinness states that this "snorting [is a] furious indignation that goes to the core of one's being."[2] Jesus hates evil and its painful effects on those He loves.

   B. How do these realizations affect you? Reflect on the truths that out of both God's love for us and His hatred of evil, He determines to redeem everything that touches His own—for our good and His glory. (See Romans 8:28 and Ephesians 1:11.)

   C. Come before the Lord now with your pain, your sorrow. Reflect on the truths that He cares, weeps with you, is in anguish with you, and is even angered by the actions of those who hurt you. How does this assurance help you today?

3. Look at Luke 10:18 and 1 Peter 5:8-9. What do you discover here about the *source* of evil?

    A. In John 8:44, how does Jesus describe Satan's character?

    B. According to Ephesians 6:11-12, what battle is now going on in our world?

    C. Think about your concept of a devil. How do these verses influence your thoughts? As you reflect on how Scripture describes Satan, how does it make you feel?

    D. What understanding do the above passages give you into the primary reason suffering exists in this world?

4. Yet do we need to fear Satan? Consider Colossians 2:13-15, 1 Peter 1:18-21, and 1 John 3:8. What did Christ do for us through His death and resurrection?

A. How do these truths free us from fear? In addition to the preceding verses, see 1 John 4:4.

B. Pause for a moment to thank God for all He has done and for His power over the Enemy. Rest in the assurance this gives you about evil.

5. Consider Galatians 5:16-21. In addition to the Evil One being an immediate source of harm today, what is a second source of suffering since the Fall—when humanity became separated from God due to sin?

A. In Mark 7:21-23, what does Jesus clearly reveal about the human condition within?

B. What understanding does this give you as to why we have problems ranging from murder, rage, and violence to jealousy, greed, and fraud?

6. Read Genesis 2:15-17 with 3:17-18. What is the third source of suffering that also resulted from the Fall? Does this give you a better understanding of the death, decay, and disease present in this world?

7. Read Jeremiah 44:2-6 for a fourth source of suffering, one that is often ignored. Explain.

    A. Before God renders judgment, He continually and repeatedly reaches out to people, desiring a change to occur. See Jeremiah 26:1-3. Even when God does finally act, what is His heart for those who have repeatedly sinned?

    B. Do you think many people ignore this source of suffering when "bad things" happen? What danger comes from not considering this possibility?

8. Evil, suffering, and death will not always be a reality. Read Revelation 21:1-5. From these verses, what is God going to do to end these "bad things"? Praise Him for this now.

9. Now read John 16:33. What hope or promise is ours, proclaimed by Jesus in these verses?

ℛEFLECTION/𝒟ISCUSSION 𝒬UESTIONS

1. What new understanding did this lesson give you as to *why* suffering touches your life? Does this understanding help you cope with your suffering? How?

2. Do you think people generally believe in the reality of an evil being? For those who do, what do they think about the Devil—what he is like and how involved he is in our world? What have your own thoughts been? How do you perceive Satan differently as a result of your discoveries in this chapter?

3. Having now explored the various sources of pain, sickness, and death, do you see God or the world in a different way? Explain.

4. What hope do you gain from seeing who Christ is, knowing what He did for you, and realizing what He will do? How do these realities help you now?

CHAPTER EIGHT

Why Doesn't God Always Protect Me?

WHEN AIRPLANES CRASHED INTO THE WORLD TRADE CENTER AND PENTAGON on September 11, 2001, our nation and much of the rest of the world was horrified. Thousands of innocent people, including devout Christians, were killed.

People asked, "Why would a good God allow this?" When we personally experience a devastating tragedy, such as a life-threatening illness or the heartbreaking loss of a child, this same question often cries agonizingly from our own hearts. We exclaim, "Why didn't the Lord protect?" Or perhaps our hearts reflect painfully, "I've lived for the Lord and done a lot for Him. Why would He let this happen to me?"

Perhaps it's not a specific event that grieves us, but difficult circumstances that keep intensifying. Day and night we cry for help, for mercy, but things only seem to get worse. "Why doesn't the Lord heed my cries? Why would He let this wrong continue?" we agonize.

Before we begin to explore these poignant issues, I first want to personally express how deeply sorry I am if you're hurting. If you're experiencing difficulty or oppression, or if you're reeling from a tragedy or loss that has broken your heart, please know I ache with you. As we explore possible "reasons" in this chapter, please know I don't mean to minimize your pain or approach this topic lightly. I grieve with you. I know that "easy answers" don't exist.

Instead, my prayer is that the truths in this chapter will help bring some comfort and hope to your hurting heart. They've helped me. In your pain, may the Lord meet you in His love and give you His peace.

1. When we're hurting and wondering where God is, we may feel that what we're experiencing is unusual.

   A. Often we think of King David as always being aware of God's presence. Yet Psalm 22:1-2 and 69:1-3 reveal a different side to David. What did he cry out in these verses? Are you surprised to read about David's feelings? Does it help to see that he did feel this way at times?

   B. Read Habakkuk 1:1-4,13-17. What issues did the prophet Habakkuk struggle with? Does this account echo your sentiments?

   C. Write your own expressions to God about any struggles you have.

2. Read Psalm 37:1-11. As you agonize over the evil in this world, what advice does David give you? What hope does he impart?

3. The Scriptures provide some understanding regarding why God doesn't always protect His own. (As you progress through this lesson, record the reasons in the blanks after each headline below.) However,

it's important to realize that many times God *does* protect us. What evidence have you seen of this?

*Reason #*1: _____

4. One reason God may not *always* protect pertains to why people would decide to establish a personal relationship with Him. If God protected His children from every difficulty or grief, why might some people choose to enter into relationship with Him? Instead, what is God's desire? Consider Matthew 22:37-38.

5. Read Romans 8:28 and Ephesians 1:11. What assurance do we receive in these verses, no matter what happens to us in life? How does this encourage you today?

*Reason #*2: _____

6. We're a part of this world, and both believers and unbelievers get "hit" with the same "storms." Jesus tells a parable depicting this in Matthew 7:24-27. When storms hit, why would God want His children alongside unbelievers who are hurting? Can you give an example?

Reason #3: _____

7. What benefit expressed in 2 Corinthians 1:3-7 results from suffering? How can it help a person going through difficult circumstances to know someone who has been through the same trial?

Reason #4: _____

8. Consider Psalm 107:1-31 (especially verses 6, 13, 19, and 28). What do these verses say about why the Lord allows difficulty to come into our lives? Have you seen this occur?

Reason #5: _____

9. Consider Jesus' dialogue with Simon Peter recorded in Luke 22:31-32. According to these verses, why does God allow some difficulties to occur?

10. Hannah Whitall Smith notes, "Here lies the secret of all that seems so mysterious in the discipline of our lives. Our loving and wise Physician has discovered in us some incipient disease that He knows will ruin us if it remains unchecked, and He is applying the remedy."[1] How have you seen the Lord use pressure or difficulty to bring to light something He wants to free you from?

11. Read Joseph's experience in Genesis 45:1-11 with 50:18-21. This illustrates how God can use even the worst things that come against us for His good plans, both individually and for the world.

    A. R. C. Sproul writes about this truth in his book *Surprised by Suffering:*

> We remember the dreadful suffering of Joseph at the hands of his brothers. Yet because of their treachery the plan of God for all of history was brought to pass. At the moment of Joseph's reconciliation with his brothers, he exclaimed, "But as for you, you meant evil against me; but God meant it for good, in order to bring it about as it is this day, to save many people alive" (Genesis 50:20). Here we see God working through evil to effect salvation. It does not make the evil of Joseph's brothers any less evil . . . But over all injustice, all pain, all suffering stands a sovereign God who works His plan of salvation over, against, and even through evil.[2]

    What hope does this give you for the circumstances of your life?

    B. Corrie ten Boom provides a well-known illustration of how God uses difficulties in His overall plan. When Corrie and many of her family were taken to a concentration camp for harboring Jews during World War II, the Lord redeemed her terrible experience in numerous ways: First, God met Corrie in her doubts and strengthened her faith. Then, she was His instrument in drawing many to Him and strengthening other believers in their faith. Afterward, the Lord used this experience in Corrie's life for a powerful ministry. Over a period of thirty-three years, she traveled in sixty-four countries speaking of how the Lord enables us to forgive, which her experience powerfully demonstrated. According to a biographer,

> [Corrie proclaimed,] "No pit is so deep that God's love is not deeper still" and "in every situation, no matter what the circumstances, Jesus is Victor!" This is a wonderful message, because it is a message of hope based on the eternal faithfulness and love of God rather than our changing circumstances. We believe Corrie because she has been to the hell of Hitler's concentration camp and come back to tell us that even in the darkest of circumstances, the Lord was with her, and Jesus was very much the Victor.[3]

12. Have you seen the Lord redeem difficulties to further His purposes in the world or to shape an individual into whom God intended that person to be? Has God worked with you in this way? If so, how?

Reason #7: _____

13. In John 15:1-4, Jesus explains another one of God's purposes through suffering. How would you describe this reason? What evidence have you seen of this?

Reason #8: _____

14. Look at 1 Peter 1:6-7. What "good" is identified that the Lord desires to bring about through difficulty? Can you think of an example of this from your own experience?

Charles Spurgeon develops this concept in his devotional *Morning and Evening:*

Our Lord in His infinite wisdom and superabundant love, sets so high a value on His people's faith that He will not screen them from those trials by which faith is strengthened. You would never have possessed the precious faith that now supports you without the fiery trial of your faith. You are a tree that never would have rooted so well if the wind had not rocked you to and fro, and made you take firm hold on the precious truths of the covenant of grace. [4]

15. If your faith is to be refined and strengthened, what do you think your responsibility is in the midst of your challenges?

Reason #9: _____

16. Consider Job 23:10, Hebrews 12:10-11, and 1 Peter 4:1-2. In addition to refining our faith, what does the Lord desire to purify? Explain.

17. In his book *Trusting God Even When Life Hurts,* Jerry Bridges addresses this aspect: "The good that God works for in our lives is conformity to the likeness of His Son. It is not necessarily comfort or happiness but conformity to Christ in ever-increasing measure in this life and in its fullness in eternity . . . The purpose of God's discipline is not to punish us but to transform us." [5]

A. How do you respond to this statement? Is being changed into Christ's likeness something you even want? Why or why not?

B. Have you ever seen the Lord use your pain for these purposes? Be specific.

Reason #10: _____

18. Read James 1:2-4. As we persevere through trials, what results in our lives? Does understanding this encourage you to persevere? How?

Reason #11: _____

19. We find the best result of going through trials in Paul's proclamation in Philippians 3:7-9. Put this in your own words. What does this say of Christ that allows Paul to claim this?

> Sheila Walsh expresses her discovery in her book *Life Is Tough but God Is Faithful:* "Even in the darkest night, the most blinding pain, the most maddening frustration—when nothing makes sense anymore—we keep going because He alone is worth it all." [6]

Reason #12: _____

20. From John 17:20-26, what additional benefit do we experience as we gain Christ and experience the process of being purified?

Oswald Chambers underscores the importance of this: "From Jesus Christ's perspective, oneness with Him, with nothing between, is the only good thing."[7] What is your response to God's incredible desire to be one with you? Meditate on this truth.

*Reason #13:*_____

21. According to John 15:8 and Ephesians 1:3-6, what other "good" results as God works in us, fills us with Himself, and draws us deeper into oneness with Him?

22. Consider yet an even higher calling along the lines of glorifying God. Oswald Chambers stated,

> *Neither is it at all satisfying to say that suffering develops character. There was more in Job's suffering than was required to develop his character, and so it is with the sanctified soul. The preface to Job's story lets in the light from the revelation point of view, namely, that God's honor was at stake, and the issue fought out in this man's soul vindicated God's honor.*[8]

In addition to bringing God glory, what does it mean to you that your struggle matters to the Lord—that His honor is at stake? Does this help you want to persevere?

23. In conclusion, we may have experiences where we simply don't perceive any good reason for why something has happened. Yet, whenever we are hurting, confused, and feel in the "dark," what are we
exhorted to do? See Isaiah 50:10.

24. Read 2 Corinthians 4:16-18. Through any time of trial, what perspective
should we try to keep?

REFLECTION/DISCUSSION QUESTIONS

1. Do the truths of this lesson provide you with any new understanding
of how God can still be good even when He doesn't totally protect us
from being touched by difficulty or attacked by Satan? Explain.

2. What new insight impressed you most from this lesson and why? How
do you think these discoveries will help you respond to difficulty differently than you have in the past? What new perspectives do the
truths of this lesson give you on the trials in your life? Explain.

3. Do you desire the good purposes of God that you explored in this
chapter? For example, do you long to know Jesus better? Is it the
desire of your heart that He be glorified in your life? If not, what do
you desire more? Express your heart honestly to God in this. If these
are your desires, ask Him to reveal Himself to you and to fulfill His
good purposes in you and for you.

4. How do you think we can keep a more "spiritual" and "eternal" perspective in the midst of our very earthly trials? What dynamics make
this difficult to do? Explain why it's critical to gain a more eternal perspective.

CHAPTER NINE

Can I Trust God to Be in Control?

C AN GOD'S PURPOSES BE THWARTED? SINCE GOD ISN'T CAPABLE OF EVIL, WE might wonder if events caused by Satan or evil people are out of God's control.

When tragedy strikes, accidents occur, or disease hits, is God surprised? Does He have to play "catch up"? We might agree that He can redeem everything that happens, but can things happen that He doesn't have any say about? If so, we truly have reason to fear. *Anything* could happen to us at *any time*. We would be at the mercy of the Enemy. Is this true?

To know a true inner peace and to not live in fear, we need to answer the question, "Is God in control of *all events* in our lives as well as in the world at *all times*?" Is He that sovereign? Could He be that powerful?

That is a critical question. Fortunately, the Bible reveals truths that equip us to handle whatever situations occur and that provide rest as we face the future.

1. When you read of tragic events occurring or hear of a disaster striking someone you know, what fears or questions overwhelm you? Can you think of a specific example of such an experience? Are you struggling with any now?

2. Do you believe that God is totally in control of this world and of our individual lives? What are your initial thoughts?

   A. What name is given the Lord in Isaiah 49:22 and 50:4-7?

      For insight into the meaning of God's sovereignty, in *Trusting God Even When Life Hurts* Jerry Bridges quotes J. I. Packer's definition of God's providence as "the unceasing activity of the Creator whereby, in overflowing bounty and goodwill, He upholds His creatures in ordered existence, guides and governs all events, circumstances, and free acts of angels and men, and directs everything to its appointed goal, for His own glory."[1] Jerry Bridges' abridged definition is, "God's providence is His constant care for and His absolute rule over all His creation for His own glory and the good of His people."[2]

   B. Do you think it's true that God is totally sovereign? What testimony does God Himself give in Isaiah 46:9-11 and Jeremiah 32:26-27? What does this mean to you?

   C. What other proof do you find in the following passages?

   Job 42:2

   Psalm 33:10-11

Proverbs 16:9

James 4:13-16

3. To explore how *complete* God's sovereignty is, consider these aspects:

   A. What does God reveal of His sovereignty in Daniel 5:22-30? Did Belshazzar know God or honor Him? What truth is stated here for all people?

   B. What does God claim in Jeremiah 27:4-7?

4. Is God completely able to carry out His plans or can the Enemy thwart God? Consider the incident concerning Ahab, an evil king of Israel. Ahab and Jehoshaphat, the good king of Judah, had united forces for battle. However, the Lord revealed through his prophet Micaiah that Ahab would be killed. To prevent this from happening, Ahab went into battle in disguise. What do you discover of God's sovereignty in the ensuing events recorded in 2 Chronicles 18:27-34?

5. Read 2 Chronicles 36:21-23 and in 1 Kings 12:8,15. What do these verses tell you about God's ability to accomplish His purposes even through people who do not know Him? What confidence does this give you?

6. Do you think any circumstance can exist that is too great for God? Read Daniel 3:16-27, the familiar incident of Shadrach, Meshach, and Abednego in the fiery furnace.

   A. What do you discover about their trust in God?

   B. Describe the overwhelming circumstances.

   C. Just how powerful was God? Record the incredible details here.

   D. As you reflect on this actual event, express your awe of God's power and greatness to Him here.

7. God's ability to fulfill His purposes even when we're completely unaware of what He's doing is illustrated in Saul's experience. As the Israelites were demanding a king, the Lord selected the young man, Saul.

A. Read 1 Samuel 9:1-17. What caused Saul to venture out? Did he have clear direction where he was going? How many areas, or territories, did Saul travel through? Put yourself in Saul's place. How easy do you think it would have been to end up in the wrong town?

i. In verses 15-17, what did the Lord reveal to Samuel?

ii. How does this scenario affect you?

B. What occurred next in 1 Samuel 10:1-7?

C. Although God had Samuel anoint Saul as king privately, the public process needed to follow for the "official" appointment of the king of Israel. According to 1 Samuel 10:20-24, what did this process involve? Who was selected out of all the people of Israel?

D. How does Saul's example encourage you? Have you seen God exhibit His sovereignty in fulfilling purposes in your life or in the life of someone you know? How?

8. What's your initial response to the following question: Do you think *any* circumstance would make it too difficult for the Lord to fulfill His purposes?

A. What did God do in the situations recorded in Numbers 22:21-35 and Acts 12:6-11?

B. What truth is clearly stated in Genesis 18:14, Matthew 19:26, and Luke 1:37?

C. How is this truth exemplified in the incidents recorded in the following verses?

Joshua 3:9-17

2 Kings 20:8-11

John 9:1-7

D. What's your response to who God is? Is He bigger than you realized and more powerful? How do your discoveries change you?

E. Does a better understanding of God's power and sovereign control help you in whatever happens in your day or in your life? If so, how?

9. Even though the Lord can work powerfully and miraculously, often He chooses to work quietly, sovereignly ordering what seem like natural circumstances. Do you think God's power is any less when He works intricately through complex natural events rather than dramatically intervening in a situation? Explain.

A. Consider the following example of how God quietly and intricately fulfilled His purposes through circumstances:

In the 1930s, Stalin ordered a purge of all Bibles and all believers. In Stavropol, Russia, this order was carried out with a vengeance. Thousands of Bibles were confiscated and multitudes of believers were sent to . . . prison camps.

Last year [1994], the CoMission sent a team to Stavropol . . . But when our team was having difficulty getting Bibles shipped from Moscow, someone mentioned the existence of a warehouse where these confiscated Bibles had been stored since Stalin's day . . . The CoMissioners asked if the Bibles could be removed and distributed again to the people of Stavropol. The answer was, "Yes!"

The next day the CoMission team returned with a truck and several hundred Russian people to help load the Bibles. One helper was a young man—a skeptical, hostile, agnostic collegian who had come only for the day's wages. As they were loading Bibles, one team member noticed that the young man had disappeared. Eventually they found him in a corner of the warehouse, weeping.

He had slipped away, hoping to quietly take a Bible for himself. What he found shook him to the core. The inside page of the Bible he picked up had the handwritten signature of his own grandmother. It had been her personal Bible! Out of the thousands of Bibles still left in that warehouse, he stole the one belonging to his grandmother.[3]

What is your response to seeing God work in such a way?

B. Can you give examples of God's sovereign control in your own life, perhaps even in a small incident in the routine of your day? Describe the intricacy of His control.

10. What is declared of God's ways in Deuteronomy 32:4 and 2 Samuel 22:31,33? When you don't understand what God is doing in a certain situation, how does understanding this help you?

11. Review Psalm 62:8. In light of the truths of God's goodness and complete sovereignty, what are we enabled to do?

12. When painful events occur, it's important to be honest in our feelings, to go to the Lord with them, and to hang on to what is true.

One young woman's experience illustrates this. In 1996, Susie Bodman Todd, at the age of 29, lost her husband, a captain in the Air Force. Killed in a plane crash, he left a two-year-old son and Susie due with their second child that next month. Following his service, Susie wrote the minister this note: "I do realize that my loss is heaven's gain, and God has honored me by using me in this way to further His perfect will. Though I cannot see His big picture, I do trust that God is in control. If I could see that picture, I know I would choose these same circumstances that so grieve me now."

The night that she'd received the news of her husband's death, she had cried to the Lord in her pain and grief. Although she besieged the Lord with questions, she sensed the Lord asking her a question: "Can you trust me to take you through this?" As she chose to trust Him and cast herself upon Him, He revealed Himself to her. Although He didn't answer her questions of why, He showed her *Who* is with her.

Susie recently said, "God is, indeed, good, and it is during our trials that He takes our head knowledge of who He is and confirms in us an indisputable heart knowledge of His perfect faithfulness . . . God truly uses all things for the good of those who love Him, who are called according to His purpose . . . God's plan is not always one we can figure out. We can, however, rest in the fact that He is sovereign, He is in control, and we can trust Him."

The "rest of the story" is that two years later, Susie married a minister. They have a . . . wonderful marriage, a loving family, and a powerful ministry. She writes, "I see now how God has prepared me for the ministry I have with my husband, Pat. Knowing that God was faithful to sustain me through the awful loss of my first husband gives me infinite confidence that He will walk me through the unending challenges of ministry and He supplies me with His precious joy and peace each step of the way."

Because God is with us when "bad things happen," we can trust Him because He is who He says He is. How is this expressed in Psalm 31:14?

13. What pain are you struggling with today? What circumstances cause you distress? Come to the Lord with them now. *As you feel the pain, allow Him to comfort you and minister to you in His love.* Ask Him to heal your hurts. Offer each to God for Him to redeem. Ask Him to accomplish the good purposes for which He's allowed this struggle. Savor Jesus' love for you. Receive His love as a healing balm for each wound.

14. We can take the following *specific, helpful steps* when something painful occurs:

A. Seek discernment. Ask yourself, "Is this event of Satan and does God want me to stand against it so it doesn't touch me? Or is the Lord allowing it for higher purposes in my life?" Seek direction in any steps God would have you take throughout the course of the trial (see 2 Chronicles 20:12).

B. Stand against Satan's purposes. No matter what the source of a trial, Satan always desires to defeat us, discourage us, destroy our faith, turn us from the Lord, and bring dishonor to Him. Bind the Enemy and actively stand against his purposes in the name of Jesus (see Ephesians 6:10-18).

C. Yield yourself and your circumstances to the Lord. Offer yourself to Him for all His good purposes (see Romans 12:1-2).

D. Stay in an abiding position. Spend time daily with the Lord, staying close to Him, even if you don't feel His presence or see any observable benefit (see John 15:1-16).

E. Keep seeking. It's okay to wrestle before the Lord with your doubts. Come to Him with your struggles. Seek truth (see Luke 11:5-13; Hebrews 11:6).

F. Hang on to facts. Hold tight to what you know to be true according to God's Word. Don't depend on how you feel or how things look (see 2 Timothy 3:16-17). Keep your eyes fixed on Jesus! Stay focused on who you know Him to be (see Hebrews 12:1-3).

G. Persevere in faith. Don't give up! You don't want to miss the good that God has for you in this trial (see James 1:2-4; 5:7-11). Remember, too, that God's honor is at stake.

H. Pray for God's purposes to be accomplished. Be proactive! Ask God to unite your will with His (see Ephesians 6:18; Philippians 4:6-7; Colossians 4:2,12). Ask for others to pray for you as well.

I. Trust. Because God is who He says He is, you can trust Him even when you don't understand what He's doing (see Psalms 31:14-15; 62:8; Isaiah 50:10; John 16:33).

J. Choose to praise Him for who you know Him to be. Praise is powerful. Praise defeats the Enemy, strengthens us, and pleases God (see Psalm 34:1; Habakkuk 3:17-18; Hebrews 13:15).

K. Keep an eternal perspective (see 2 Corinthians 4:16-18).

REFLECTION/DISCUSSION QUESTIONS

1. As you reflect on this lesson, what discoveries were especially meaningful or helpful to you?

2. Did God become "bigger" to you through this study? In what ways? Were you aware of how complete God's sovereignty is? Did areas of His control surprise you? What aspects of God's sovereignty particularly encouraged you? Explain.

3. Does it seem that the sovereign God existed in the past, but that He's not as active today? Do you think we blindly go about our routines

and miss what He's doing? How can we become more alert to the Lord and His activity in our days?

4. How does being aware of God's total control help you with any fears you may have for your own life or for those you love? How do the truths of this lesson help you regarding any painful events in the past? Apply these truths to your present and your future as well.

CHAPTER TEN

Do My Prayers Really Make a Difference?

SINCE GOD IS SOVEREIGN, DOES IT MATTER IF WE PRAY? HOW DO PRAYER AND God's sovereignty fit together? This is important to understand if we want to be effective in our prayers.

Perhaps your own experience has discouraged you when it comes to prayer. Maybe you've prayed and prayed, yet nothing seems to happen. Is prayer simply a spiritual exercise with no guarantee that it will result in any great effects?

The Bible includes many promises about the power of prayer. But if we're not experiencing that reality, it's important to discover what we're missing.

Although prayer is about far more than power, this issue of effective prayer is one that many people question. When we consider God's sovereignty and the reality of our own pain, we want to know: Does prayer make a difference?

1. What initial thoughts do you have regarding prayer and how effective it is? What has your experience been? Do you think it makes a difference if you pray? What do you struggle with about prayer?

2. Scripture has a lot to say about prayer.

   A. What *directives* regarding prayer do you discover in the following verses?

   Luke 18:1

   Ephesians 6:18

   Colossians 4:2

   B. What *promises* are we given in the following Scriptures?

   Jeremiah 33:3

   Luke 11:9-10

   Philippians 4:6-7

C. From these verses, what *evidence* do you find that prayer is powerful?

1 Kings 18:36-39

Daniel 9:20-23

Acts 4:29-31

3. How do you think God's sovereignty fits into the context of power in prayer? Is His sovereignty a discouraging factor or an encouraging one? For insight, consider Jerry Bridges' comments from his book *Trusting God Even When Life Hurts*:

> The disciples believed in the sovereignty of God. But God's sovereignty to them was a reason and an encouragement to pray. They believed because God was sovereign He was able to answer their prayers ... Prayer assumes the sovereignty of God. If God is not sovereign, we have no assurance that He is able to answer our prayers. Our prayers would become nothing more than wishes. But while God's sovereignty, along with His wisdom and love, is the foundation of our trust in Him, prayer is the expression of that trust.[1]

For an illustration of these truths, read Daniel 10:12-14. What occurred in these verses? How was prayer proven to be powerful? How did God's sovereignty enter in?

4. Daniel's experience reveals the importance of prayer when it comes to spiritual warfare. In previous chapters, we explored the real existence of Satan and his attempts to defeat God's purposes. But God equips us for this battle. Review Ephesians 6:10-18.

   A. According to Luke 10:19, what power and authority does Jesus desire for us to exercise in this battle?

   B. Wesley Duewel states in *Mighty Prevailing Prayer*: "Christ has already won the victory, and Satan is already defeated. From that position of power and authority, command Satan to leave. By virtue of Christ's victory, bind Satan, your enemy, by the power of Jesus' name."[2] Duewel also proclaims, "Prevailing prayer unites you with all the forces of heaven."[3] Does the reminder of Christ's victory and power over Satan encourage you to keep prevailing in prayer? With this assurance, bind Satan now from any involvement he might have in circumstances you've been praying for.

5. Read 2 Corinthians 10:4-5. What do you discover about utilizing the power of prayer?

   A. Strongholds can exist that prevent people from growing in the Lord. Some of these strongholds can arise from anger, bitterness, unforgiveness, fear, guilt, rebellion against God, unbelief, or willfulness. How is one stronghold explained in 2 Corinthians 2:10-11 and in Ephesians 4:26-27,30-32?

B. If someone faces a continual problem or "just can't get past" something, that's a clue a stronghold may exist. If you've been praying for a person or situation for a length of time with little or no apparent results, ask the Lord if a stronghold needs to be demolished. Pray for all strongholds to be demolished in the name of Jesus, then ask for the Spirit to be released to accomplish God's purposes. List those prayer needs here and take time to pray in this way. Persevere until you see results.

6. Read John 16:23-24 and 1 John 5:14-15. In addition to defeating enemy involvement, what do these verses promise as another dimension of powerful prayer?

A. Do you have questions about this being true? This is an aspect of prayer where many people get confused and discouraged. Reread the preceding verses. What conditions do these passages list as part of praying in this way?

B. To understand what Jesus means when He urges us to ask in His name, consider John 15:7-8. Do you think that asking in His name means more than simply *using* His name? Explain.

C. For further insight, read Jeremiah 23:16-22 with Lamentations 3:37.

    i. What were the prophets doing in the days of Jeremiah? Do we do something similar when we pray?

    ii. What, instead, does God exhort us to do?

D. Read Joshua 5:13-15. When the commander of the Lord's army (the pre-incarnate Christ) appeared to Joshua, what lesson does He reveal regarding prayer? Describe the contrast between Joshua's initial approach and the attitude he concluded with. Explain how you think this incident reveals a key to powerful prayer.

E. Regarding any matters on your heart today, seek the Lord's mind, will, and purposes in each. Whenever He reveals His will in a matter, ask powerfully in His name. This releases His Spirit to accomplish His good purposes.

7. When we don't know how to pray, or we fear our wills may be contrary to God's, should we not pray at all? What do you discover from Jesus' example in Mark 14:32-36?

A. Would you rather not pray and take what comes, or pray and accept what comes? Explain.

B. Read Proverbs 3:5-6 and Isaiah 55:9. What encouragement do you find in these verses? How do these truths help you trust God?

8. Study Romans 8:26-27. What assurance do these verses provide if you don't know what to ask in prayer or can't verbalize your feelings?

9. What additional insight does James 4:1-3 give into the concept of power in prayer? Have you seen this to be true? How?

10. What does James 5:16-18 clearly state about prayer? As you read the description and example of Elijah, how are you encouraged? Explain.

11. It always helps to read what others have discovered about the power of prayer. Read these examples.

> George Müller, who established orphanages in England in the mid-1800s, many times experienced God removing obstacles through prayer. One such incident happened when days of intense fog kept his ship from reaching the port where he was to speak. Müller knelt with the ship's unbelieving captain and prayed—and by the time he had finished praying, the fog was gone.[4]
>
> Hudson Taylor, medical missionary and founder of the China Inland Mission, also knew the secret of prayer: "The morning watch was one of the great secrets of his close walk with God and of his ever-increasing faith." In his ministry,

Taylor experienced power in prayer and routinely saw that "it was possible to move man through God by prayer alone."[5]

What impact do these examples have on you?

12. Now that you've learned more about the importance of prayer and its powerful results, examine your schedule. Do you desire to spend greater lengths of time getting to know the Lord, fellowshiping with Him, and praying? Seek God's direction about what you can eliminate or rearrange in your days. Place those times on your calendar and protect them. Over time, you'll notice the Lord drawing you closer to Himself and increasing your effectiveness in all areas of life and prayer. Review Jesus' promises in John 15:4-8.

13. In closing, A. W. Tozer challenges us in our faith: "The heavenly birth [is] not an end but an inception, for now begins the glorious pursuit, the heart's happy exploration of the infinite riches of the Godhead. That is where we begin, I say, but where we stop no man has yet discovered, for there is in the . . . mysterious depths of the Triune God neither limit nor end."[6] What's your hope as you pursue Christ? Express to the Lord everything that's filling your heart, and keep your eyes fixed on Him.

REFLECTION/DISCUSSION QUESTIONS

1. If you had to explain to a friend how you reconcile the power of prayer with God's sovereignty, what would you say? What insights from this study did you find especially helpful?

2. Did you gain new insights regarding prayer from this lesson? Summarize them.

3. What are we saying to God when we insist on our own way in prayer? As we think about God's character and the eternal value of His purposes, why would we not want His will?

4. Regarding the concept of powerful prayer, do you think people are willing to take the time necessary to remain close to Christ in order to discern His mind and will? Why or why not? Do people seem to want the benefits without nurturing the relationship? If so, why do you think that is?

5. In what new ways are you challenged now to grow? Be specific. How will you arrange to spend more time with the Lord? You might want to ask someone to help hold you accountable in this area.

A Personal Word

"WEEPING MAY REMAIN FOR A NIGHT, BUT *rejoicing comes in the morning*" (Psalm 30:5, emphasis added). Throughout my "dark night," I longed for the "morning." The promise of the joy that was still ahead kept me going: the joy of knowing the Lord better, the joy of becoming increasingly one with Him, the joy of experiencing a greater fullness of His Spirit, the joy of living more effectively for Him, and the joy of pleasing and glorifying Him more fully.

While the night I suffered through felt long and dark, God sometimes kept me going with encouraging words from Scripture. One of these was Isaiah 51:3: "The LORD will surely comfort Zion and will look with compassion on all her ruins; he will make her deserts like Eden, her wastelands like the garden of the LORD. Joy and gladness will be found in her, thanksgiving and the sound of singing." These words gave me hope.

I found inspiration at the conclusion of Psalm 30. David closes with this declaration: "You turned my wailing into dancing; you removed my sackcloth and clothed me with joy, that my heart may sing to you and not be silent. O LORD my God, I will give you thanks forever" (30:11-12). I trusted that someday this would be my experience as well.

In addition to His Word, God used other books to encourage me. One that was especially helpful was Watchman Nee's *The Normal Christian Life*, particularly for the insights he gained from his own dark night.

> The difficulty with many of us is that dark night . . . The temptation is always to try to help God by taking things back ourselves; but remember, there must be . . . a full night in darkness. It cannot be hurried; he knows what he is doing . . .
>
> Of course, I cannot tell you how long he will take, but in principle I think it is quite safe to say this, that there will be a definite

period when he will keep you there. It will seem as though nothing is happening; as though everything you valued is slipping from your grasp. There confronts you a blank wall with no door in it. Seemingly everyone else is being blessed and used, while you yourself have been passed by and are losing out. Lie quiet. All is in darkness, but it is only for a night. It must indeed be a full night, but that is all. Afterward, you will find that everything is given back to you in glorious resurrection; and nothing can measure the difference between what was before and what now is![1] (Emphasis mine.)

"Resurrection morning" does come! Gratefully and joyfully, I experience this now. Nothing has really changed about my circumstances. But I am different. Although I still have times of hurting, morning is gradually breaking. Satan has not won. My faith was not destroyed. Although I experience the fulfillment of many promises, I still wait on God for others. But a *difference* exists in me.

What's different? I know Jesus better. I love Him more. The deeper oneness I experience with Him is precious. Christ is more fully my life, my joy, my delight. He is my Beloved. And my faith is stronger; I know without a doubt that *God is who He says He is.*

In addition, I'm more sensitive to the Holy Spirit, which results both in a more effective prayer life and in simply living more fully in Him each day. I also see the Lord working more powerfully in all He calls me to do. My worship of God is richer. My peace is deeper. My joy overflows. I have discovered: God is enough! Jesus is my delight.

But of course, He's not through with me. Even that is a joy to me. Therefore, I continue to "press on to take hold of that for which Christ Jesus took hold of me" (Philippians 3:12). Christ is worth it all. With joy I celebrate Him—and press on to know Him better. The best is yet to come!

Notes

CHAPTER TWO: WHOM CAN I GO TO FOR TRUTH?

1. Josh McDowell, *More Than a Carpenter* (Carol Stream, Ill.: Tyndale, 1977), pp. 25-27.

2. Dr. D. Martyn Lloyd-Jones, *Authority* (Chicago: InterVarsity, 1958), p. 21.

CHAPTER THREE: CAN I TRUST GOD'S WORD?

1. John R. W. Stott, *The Authority of the Bible* (Downers Grove, Ill.: InterVarsity, 1974), p. 30.

2. Dr. D. Martyn Lloyd-Jones, *Authority* (Chicago: InterVarsity, 1958), pp. 49, 38.

3. Josh McDowell, *The New Evidence That Demands a Verdict* (Nashville, Tenn.: Nelson, 1999), pp. 12-13.

4. Oswald Chambers, *God's Workmanship* (Grand Rapids, Mich.: Discovery House Publishers, 1997), pp. 48-49.

5. Warren W. Wiersbe, compiler, *The Best of* A. W. *Tozer* (Camp Hill, Pa.: Christian Publications, 1995), pp. 20-21, 26.

6. Lloyd-Jones, p. 35.

CHAPTER FOUR: "LORD, DO YOU LOVE ME?"

1. Henri J. M. Nouwen, *Life of the Beloved* (New York: Crossroad Publishing, 1992), pp. 45, 49.

2. Nouwen, p. 109.

3. Jerry Bridges, *Transforming Grace* (Colorado Springs, Colo.: NavPress, 1991), pp. 12, 33, 53, 87.

*C*HAPTER *F*IVE: "LORD, DO YOU KNOW EVERY DETAIL OF MY LIFE—AND DO YOU CARE?"

1. J. I. Packer, *Knowing God* (Downers Grove, Ill.: InterVarsity, 1973), p. 113.

*C*HAPTER *S*IX: "LORD, ARE YOU REALLY GOOD?"

1. Billy Graham, *Hope for the Troubled Heart* (Nashville, Tenn.: Word, 1995), pp. 44–45.

*C*HAPTER *S*EVEN: WHY DO BAD THINGS HAPPEN TO ME?

1. Joni Eareckson Tada and Steve Estes, *When God Weeps* (Grand Rapids, Mich.: Zondervan, 1997), p. 14.

2. Os Guinness, The Trinity Forum, "Riding the Storm: Making Sense of Life in a Time of Evil and Suffering," conference lecture tape, McLean, Va., Sept. 5, 2001.

*C*HAPTER *E*IGHT: WHY DOESN'T GOD ALWAYS PROTECT ME?

1. Hannah Whitall Smith, *God Is Enough* (Grand Rapids, Mich.: Zondervan, 1986), p. 185.

2. R. C. Sproul, *Surprised by Suffering* (Carol Stream, Ill.: Tyndale House, 1989), pp. 49–50.

3. Carole C. Carlson, *Corrie ten Boom—Her Life, Her Faith* (Old Tappan, N.J.: Revell, 1983), p. 212.

4. Charles H. Spurgeon, *Morning and Evening* (Grand Rapids, Mich.: Zondervan, 1980), Sept. 3, evening.

5. Jerry Bridges, *Trusting God Even When Life Hurts* (Colorado Springs, Colo.: NavPress, 1988), pp. 120–121.

6. Sheila Walsh, *Life Is Tough but God Is Faithful* (Nashville, Tenn.: Nelson, 1999), p. 23.

7. Oswald Chambers, *My Utmost for His Highest* (Grand Rapids, Mich.: Discovery House Publishers, 1992), Sept. 28.

8. Oswald Chambers, *God's Workmanship* (Grand Rapids, Mich.: Discovery House Publishers, 1997), p. 166.

CHAPTER NINE: CAN I TRUST GOD TO BE IN CONTROL?

1. Jerry Bridges, *Trusting God Even When Life Hurts* (Colorado Springs, Colo.: NavPress, 1988), p. 25.

2. Bridges, p. 25.

3. "An Answered Prayer from Stalin's Time," *The Chariot* (a newsletter of CoMission), First Quarter 1995, vol. 2, no. 1, p. 1.

CHAPTER TEN: DO MY PRAYERS REALLY MAKE A DIFFERENCE?

1. Jerry Bridges, *Trusting God Even When Life Hurts* (Colorado Springs, Colo.: NavPress, 1988), p. 107.

2. Wesley Duewel, *Mighty Prevailing Prayer* (Grand Rapids, Mich.: Zondervan, 1990), p. 107.

3. Duewel, p. 58.

4. Colin Whittaker, *Seven Guides to Effective Prayer* (Bloomington, Minn.: Bethany House, 1987), pp. 15-16.

5. Whittaker, pp. 83, 55.

6. Warren W. Wiersbe, compiler, *The Best of* A. W. *Tozer* (Camp Hill, Pa.: Christian Publications, 1995), pp. 14-15.

EPILOGUE: A PERSONAL WORD

1. Watchman Nee, *The Normal Christian Life* (Wheaton, Ill.: Tyndale, 1977), pp. 264-265.

Author

KIRKIE MORRISSEY GRADUATED WITH A BACHELOR'S DEGREE FROM WHEATON College in 1963. She speaks at conferences, both locally and nationally, and teaches a women's Bible study as well as other classes and seminars.

After college she served on Young Life staff in Tacoma, Washington. She also coordinated neighborhood Bible studies for ten years under the auspices of Young Life, writing the material and training the leaders.

Kirkie has written nine books, four of which are currently in print: *A Great Cloud of Witnesses* and *Fix Your Eyes on Jesus: Running the Race Marked Out for YOU!* (Cook), and *At Jesus' Feet* and *The Responsive Heart* (NavPress).

She has been married to her husband, Terry, for thirty-six years and has three sons, three daughters-in-law, and seven grandchildren. Kirkie loves being with family, lunching with friends, reading, hiking, and savoring gourmet coffee.

THREE MORE MOTIVATIONAL RESOURCES FOR WOMEN.

Becoming a Woman of Excellence

Society beckons us to succeed—to achieve excellence in our appearance, our earning power, and our family life. This Bible study will help you discover what you should be striving for as you look to God's excellence as a model.
(Cynthia Heald)

Six Keys to Lasting Friendships

In today's busy world, the need for friendship is as strong as ever. Discover from Jesus' life how to build new relationships and strengthen the ones you already have.
(Carol Kent and Karen Lee-Thorp)

My Soul's Journey

This guided journal uses the combination of encouraging text, thought-provoking questions, and inspiring topic ideas as a springboard for you to put your deepest thoughts and feelings down on paper.
(Carol Kent and Karen Lee-Thorp)

To get your copies, visit your local bookstore, call 1-800-366-7788, or log on to www.navpress.com. Ask for a FREE catalog of NavPress products. Offer #BPA.